Grace

Amy Gearing

Presentation by *BookLeaf Publishing*

Web: www.bookleafpub.com

E-mail: info@bookleafpub.com

ISBN: 9789357441513

First edition 2023

For my dad

ACKNOWLEDGEMENT

I wrote my first poem when I was six years old and my dad called me a poet. He would get a chuckle out of this.

Grace

Grace doesn't tiptoe through life
She walks tall with a steady stride
Chin pointed high

Grace doesn't hold her breath
She inhales the air, strong and deep
Blows it out

She does not whisper, never shouts
Grace's voice rings clear and dignified
 Anticipating your response

Grace feels all things, never numb
Her emotions are clear
Passionate and unapologetic

You see her coming
Cannot wait to greet her
Listen with rapt attention
Feel the warmth of Grace's embrace

I Tried to Write a Poem

I tried to write a poem about all the love I feel,
about the times I miss,
and the things I need, that only you can give

I tried to write a poem about all the love I feel,
about the happy times
and scary things, and advice that you should
give

I tried to write a poem about all the love I feel,
but I cannot write it
and there are not enough words, to say what I'd
give

to have you here with me.

Do You See Me?

Do you see me?
I sit in a back pew of the church,
Tissues crumpled in my hand
Friends gathered around
Tears escape from every eye.
Standing on tiptoe
Searching for a peak
I watch you

I find you across the court
It's been years, but you take your place

Do you see me?
Tears cloud my vision as I remember
All this time later
Your deep sorrow
I can't breathe
Yet I watch you

Once more we meet
You walk through my line of sight
I'm caught off guard
You see me
You smile
You share your strength
I soak it up and smile back
You saw me all along

Embrace Me

5

Arms of pink morning skies engulf me
As I walk with comfort and ease
Breathe in breathe out
Warm air kisses my cheeks

Arms of pink evening skies embrace me
As I walk with weariness and lethargy
Breathe in breathe out
Cool air kisses my cheeks
Carries me home

Past Present Future

Books stacked up behind me
Holding on to my past
Joys, sorrows, history
Follow me always

Collide into me when I stop moving
I can't push them back
I can't fight them
They are too strong
I relent

Books stacked up ahead of me
Leading me onward
To the future I work for
To the future I long for
To the future I move towards

I Am Ready

I didn't know such sadness existed
I didn't know the depths of loneliness one could
feel
I didn't know the evilness of fear
I didn't know a heart could break,
And then, before fully repairing,
Break again and again and again
Until it was shattered
Seemingly beyond repair.

I am ready
For my overabundance of joy
For my connection after connection after
connection
For my plethora of contentment
For my heart to repair to wholeness

With patience and drudgery
And love and love and love
Send my your grace
I am ready

Never Letting Go

I want to wrap you up and hold you tight
Arms aching from the pressure
Never letting go

Instead I settle
I'll take the murmured platitudes, painful to utter
The hearts overhead
The messages sent during late night hours
Read with a speeding pulse and sleepy eyes
Broad shoulders shocking me
Towering over me.

I'll wait until you are ready and willing
For me to wrap you up and hold you tight
Arms aching from the pressure
Never letting go

Baby Bird

baby bird with broken wing
lays upon its side

chirps of pain sound from parched beak
chills quake tender bones

I gently stroke the feathers
with my trembling hands

nothing else to offer but
a wish and a kiss

I circle my arms around
to protect and mend

heal yourself, baby bird
for only you can

Night Time

Nighttime is the worst
Wild hair wrapping my face, blocking my sight
The branches reach out to strangle me
I want to die but I don't
Voices screaming remain unheard
Heart beating fast, counts breaths that can't
escape

Nighttime is the best
Full moon glows through windows left ajar
Wind whispering through branches, swaying
leaves
that flutter gently to the ground
Calmness overcomes me
Heartbeat slows
I see your face, and drift to a peaceful sleep

Fire

12

Red ball of fire
Encroaches on blackened sky
We try to fight it back
We try to prepare for the inevitable
Please spare us
We lay ourselves down and let it roll over
Knowing we cannot survive

See Her

See her.
open your eyes
turn your head
she is right there in front of you
she is love
and beauty
and strength
and wholeness
but if you cannot see her,
I will keep her for myself

Keep Moving Forward

15

Don't turn around
Don't look back
Keep walking forward
Through the dark.

No backward glance
No glimpse across the shoulder
Keep you breathing even
Along the dampened road

Look straight ahead
Eyes opened wide
Right in front of you
Don't turn around

You will get there
The white light beckons
Keep a steady pace
There's no need to run

Don't let them chase you
Or pull you back with them
Clear and confident
Keep moving forward

Snowy Night

she slips sideways on the snow covered road,
wetness seeping into her clothes
soft piles surround
tilts her head back and lets swirling icicles tickle
her tongue
white against the dark moonlit night
celebrating the stillness and solitude
she laughs

No More to Give

17

Cold, dreary, never-ending days
filled with so much to do
Dark and rainy
leave a chill in your bones that will not escape
Demands and deadlines
dates circled on the calendar
Limbs pulling in all directions
Let me rest
Let me sleep
I have no more to give

I Fought

Eyes wide open with no tears to shed
Air, which lungs cannot expel
Screams in my head no one else can hear
Frozen in my tracks, my body cannot move

I hear voices screaming,
"Fight!"
I fight.
I fight.
I fight.

Tears spill over, forming rivers in the ground
Breath restored at rapid pace
Shrieks so loud the birds echo and fly
Legs race away so far I soar

I fought.
I won.

Body

Curves I used to hate, I now caress
Scars I once would hide, I now display
Brokenness that never healed, viewed with
shame is now revered.
I dress it up
And feed it well
And move it every which way.
We work,
we play,
we train,
we rest.
It is my miracle
I make no apologies,
not one excuse
I treat it with Grace

She Sleeps

Curled in a ball
On satin sheets
With measured breaths
And peaceful dreams;
With moon hung high
And soft winds outside
Cool breeze flows in,
Soundly she sleeps

Grace Rains Down

Grace rains down
It pours over our heads
We raise umbrellas to deflect it away
We hide from it

Refuse it
This God- given kindness we will not see
Cannot bear to accept
Fight it and push it away

Peel off your layers
Come out of hiding
Let the grace fall over you
Feel the embrace
The beauty
The wonder
Let God's grace cover you whole
Wash the horrors away with grace